<The Power of CODING/>

The Power of Java

Aidan M. Ryan

Cavendish
Square
New York

Published in 2018 by Cavendish Square Publishing, LLC
243 5th Avenue, Suite 136, New York, NY 10016

Copyright © 2018 by Cavendish Square Publishing, LLC

First Edition

Library of Congress Cataloging-in-Publication Data

Names: Ryan, Aidan M.
Title: The power of Java / Aidan M. Ryan.
Description: New York : Cavendish Square, 2018. | Series: The power of coding |
Includes bibliographical references and index. | Audience: Grades 9-12.
Identifiers: ISBN 9781502629425 (library bound) | ISBN 9781502634177 (pbk.) | ISBN 9781502629432 (ebook)
Subjects: LCSH: JavaScript (Computer program language)--Juvenile literature.
Classification: LCC QA76.73.J39 R93 2018 | DDC 005.2'762--dc23

Editorial Director: David McNamara
Editor: Caitlyn Miller
Copy Editor: Rebecca Rohan
Associate Art Director: Amy Greenan
Designer: Alan Sliwinski
Production Assistant: Karol Szymczuk

```
rt java.security..;
rt protection;

lic class Client {
blic void sendAuth
outputstream outs
DataOutputStream
long t1 = (new D
double q1 = Math
byte[] protecte
long t2 = (new
double q2 = Ma
byte[] protec
out.writeUTF
out.writeInt
out.write(p
out.flush(

blic sta
string h
int por
string
string
socke

clie
clie
```

<Chapter One/>

The History of Java

B etween the time you wake up and the time you fall back asleep, you probably watch TV, browse the **internet**, use apps on a smartphone, and connect to Wi-Fi through a router—and most of these things you'll do multiple times in a day. In the same day, you might swipe a credit card, use a Kindle or other e-reader, take cash out of an ATM, pay for parking at an electronic meter, print something, and set or disarm a home security system. You don't usually spend much time thinking about all these things. Some of the

Opposite: Your text messages may be short, but millions of lines of code are working behind each one.

actions are automatic, they're so much a part of daily life in the twenty-first century.

But none of this would be possible if, decades ago, a few wildly inventive people hadn't dreamed about groundbreaking new ways humans could interact with machines and with each other. They dreamed that instead of just using computers to create plain old text and pictures that didn't move, and using the internet to share these, people could interact with responsive computers. That could mean something as simple as clicking and dragging files across a screen to your desktop's "recycling bin," or something as complex as running an airplane's control systems. A **computer programming language**—a language that humans write, but that only machines can "speak"—is what makes all this possible. There are hundreds of these languages, and all have different strengths and functions. One that powers cable TV, internet routers, smartphone apps, and household electronics is called Java. Java has shaped the modern world, and whether you realize it or not, you use it every day.

Java in Your World: Smartphones and Pokémon Go

The summer of 2016 was *hot*. According to American climate scientists, 2016 was the hottest year ever recorded on Earth, and July and August were the hottest months of that year. Usually temperatures that high keep people indoors, in the comfort of air conditioning, or at least close to fans and cold drinks. But that summer, many people chose to spend more time outdoors.

Through July and August, almost everywhere you went outside, you'd see people walking back and forth over sidewalks and lawns, in no apparent pattern, heads bent down to smartphone screens. There was something hotter than the temperatures that summer: a new, simple smartphone app called *Pokémon Go*.

On July 6, video game company Nintendo, along with game development company Niantic, released a game that would reboot a twenty-year-old brand called Pokémon and at the same time change the way both kids and adults interacted with their phones and with each other. It wasn't just a fad—it was a phenomenon. The game became the fastest-growing app—or **application**, a name for any computer program, from massive games to tiny tools like calculators—in the history of smartphones. Today, it stands as the most popular smartphone game ever. Only six months after it launched, the app had earned its makers $1 billion.

Digital characters hovered over real tables and chairs, seemed to hide behind trees and bushes, and lurked in lakes and graveyards, ready to be captured.

The potential dangers of playing *Pokémon Go* became clear soon after it was released. This sign was posted in New York City the summer of 2016.

Players could train their Pokémon to fight. The winners of these battles were rewarded with control of virtual "gyms" scattered around the real world—over places like libraries, schools, parks, and coffee shops. It didn't matter what brand of smartphone or tablet you had: anyone could play. The game was popular, and sometimes dangerous; some players were so distracted that they broke bones, crashed cars, or were robbed. One newspaper reported that players caused over 110,000 road accidents in just ten days.

Pokémon Go was a phenomenon, but it wasn't a revolution. Some players dropped off and moved on to new games. While it remains somewhat popular today, it isn't making headlines. Really, all the fuss over *Pokémon Go*—the billion dollars, hundreds of millions of downloads, and hundreds of thousands of accidents—was the result of an effort to bring together many different technologies across many different computer platforms.

To do this, the designers of the game took old technologies and used them in new ways. One important tool was **GPS**. GPS, or "Global Positioning System," uses satellites to track the movement of devices on Earth. It wasn't a new technology—most phones were already made to be tracked this way. The game also depended on a phone's built-in camera. This was old, too: manufacturers introduced cameras to flip phones more than ten years before people started using things like Snapchat and Instagram. (Fun fact: the word "selfie" was first used in 2002 in an Australian online forum, but it took a full decade to become popular everywhere. Oxford English Dictionaries named "selfie" their word of the year in 2013, and Merriam-Webster added the word to its dictionary the following year.) But the makers of *Pokémon Go* brought these older technologies—GPS and built-in cameras, as well as others—together. Because of this, they were able to place the collectible characters from their Pokémon franchise into the "real world." To bring all these systems together, the developers had to use a "language" that could speak with all those other technologies: the GPS, the camera, the touch screen, the phone's operating system, and the game's servers. Not only did the language Java make all this possible, but the very belief that vastly different computing systems can and ought to be able to work together seamlessly grew out of a revolution in thinking, a revolution in which Java played a pivotal part.

Modern Computing: A Brief History of the Web and the Internet

This story goes back to 1991. This was a year of quiet turning points. The Cold War ended, as the Soviet Union broke up into fifteen separate nations. The United States began its continuing military involvement in the Middle East with Operation Desert Storm. The popular video game character Sonic the Hedgehog debuted, as did the Super Nintendo Entertainment System, or SNES, and two German tourists discovered a three-thousand-year-old mummy and named him Ötzi. Then, on August 6, the British scientist Tim Berners-Lee released something called the **World Wide Web** to the public, and life as we know it was radically changed.

While we sometimes use the words interchangeably, the internet and the web are two different things. The internet refers to a system of computers—machines that

Computers today are much slimmer than those from earlier decades, like this IBM notebook from the 1990s.

carry out arithmetical or logical tasks automatically—connected all over the world. This system began with US government research in the 1960s. Scientists and members of the military had been using precursors to modern computers for centuries, but these machines were becoming increasingly complex. Researchers in California, say, wanted a way to access data held in Wisconsin—or anywhere else. The US Department of Defense established rules that allowed different computers to use radio waves and electric and fiber optic cables to communicate, exchanging data and commands. By the 1980s, military and academic communities were widely using this limited internet.

In January of 1991, English scientist Tim Berners-Lee, who worked at the nuclear research facility CERN in Switzerland, introduced the World Wide Web, an information space using the internet to identify, organize, and link text documents, and eventually images, audio, and video. At first, this was only available to scientists at research institutions, but by August of that year, the general public had access. Today, when you use a browser like Safari, Internet Explorer, Firefox, or Google Chrome, you're using a tool invented to give you access to that same web. The information space designed to help scientists share data now lets you post photos to Facebook, buy tickets to concerts, browse Pinterest and Amazon, upload music to SoundCloud, and make memes.

New Language for a New Frontier

Each new advance and innovation pushed programmers to dream up more and more daring uses for these powerful new technologies. To make computers "do" anything at all, though, you need a way of commanding them—and to command, you need a language to carry that command. We call this computer programming.

Whether you know only one language, or two, or several, you probably know what it's like to use different "languages" for different situations. You speak one way to your teacher, one way on the basketball court or baseball diamond, one way to your parents, and another way to your friends or siblings. Computers work the same way: they "talk" in different languages to get different things done. Individual computers operate on something called **machine language**, which consists of **strings** of **binary code**. "Binary" just refers to something that has two parts; in the case of computers, binary code is made up of long strings of 1s and 0s. As you might imagine, it would be very hard (and time-consuming!) for a human to give a computer any complex directions using binary codes. Additionally, different computers read binary code in different ways. To make programming easier, and to help computers communicate with each other, computer pioneers created **assembly language**, which introduced letters and recognizable words. This allowed programmers to refer to blocks of data by name, and to deliver short, easily expressible commands, rather than stringing together long lines of binary digits.

Programmers still use assembly language for certain tasks, but as humans started to use computers to draw on vaster and vaster sets of data, and to perform more complicated functions, researchers realized they would need even more sophisticated languages. Today, there are more than two thousand computer languages.

You might recognize some of the names: some of the more popular are C, C++, PHP, and JavaScript. Java is one of the most popular, powerful, and influential of these languages.

The Green Team

In 1991, the same year that the World Wide Web was opened up to public access, programmers at a company called Sun Microsystems, Inc. began work on what would eventually become Java. The top executives at Sun knew a change was coming to computer culture, and they wanted to get out ahead of it. They took some of their best programmers and gave them an enormous challenge: anticipate the next big trends in computers and build something to take advantage of them. These thirteen employees were called "the Green Team," and they set up shop in Menlo Park, California, away from the main Sun offices. They even cut off most regular communication with the rest of the company for eighteen months, as they worked day and night trying to predict the future.

Their first idea was that computers would eventually play a bigger role in digital entertainment. The Green Team imagined people using handheld devices with animated touchscreens to control their TVs. They built a device called the Star Seven (*7) that did exactly this. They were right, but they were about twenty years ahead of their time. Today, you can program your TV to record shows from your phone, video game systems have taken over home entertainment, and streaming services like Hulu and Netflix give consumers more choice in how they use their televisions and their time. You don't just flick through channels when you turn on a TV—you search for exactly what you want, you can look at trailers and previews, and you can even use your voice to deliver commands. Back in the early 1990s, cable companies weren't too keen on giving up so much control to their consumers, and video-on-demand was just in its infancy. The *7 didn't take off, but the technology that made it possible did.

The *7 device used a new programming language. The lead Green Team developer, James Gosling, invented the language and named it Oak, after a tree outside his office window. But cable companies weren't interested in their product. The team members needed to find another use for this new technology, and the language that powered it. To come up with an answer, they met at a ski resort, the Inn at Squaw Creek, near Lake Tahoe in California.

By this point, developers were using the internet to store and share text, graphics, and even video. To do this, they used a language called HTML, hypertext markup language. This is the language behind most of the web pages that you use. HTML lets programmers create pages displaying different kinds of text and graphics and also lets them place links to other web pages. HTML can transfer information between different devices—so you can display and navigate web pages written in HTML whether you're using a Mac, a PC, your phone, or another device. However, a user can't do much to interact with a web page written only using HTML.

"The Network Is the Computer"

The Green Team, which switched its name to FirstPerson, got back to work, shifting focus from television to the internet. By 1993, the introduction of a web browser called **Mosaic** had started to bring more and more casual users to the web. The name Mosaic came from the art form of using many tiny pieces of glass, marble, or other colored materials to make a bigger picture. This captured the spirit—and one of the challenges—of the early web. Sharing information and commands among machines was difficult because the machines themselves were different: each type of machine "spoke" its own language, and there was not yet a language that would make it easy and efficient for different types of machines, or operating systems, to communicate. Anything that could bring all these different machines—and users—together, whether a web browser or a programming language, would work like a mosaic, using thousands and eventually billions of individuals to make up one massive, colorful whole: a network.

The developers at Sun Microsystems started thinking about the internet in a new way. They realized that the internet was becoming a lot like what they'd hoped the cable companies would make, an interactive multimedia network. Scott McNealy, the co-founder, chair, and CEO of Sun, came up with a new slogan for the company: "The network is the computer." It sounds a bit like a riddle, but it makes a lot of sense if you think about it. People tended to think of the first personal computers, or PCs, as labor-saving devices, the way you might think of your toaster, blender, or lawn mower. But "connecting" all the toasters in the world wouldn't make them any more powerful. Perhaps you could arrange a million toasters to make toast at the same time. That would be cool, but not very practical. Computers, McNealy and others started to realize, were different.

One PC was powerful, but a network of millions and later billions of PCs would have literally infinite potential. Instead of putting the PC at the heart of the computing world, Sun Microsystems encouraged its employees and customers to think of the network first. The real power wasn't in the personal computer, but in the fact that billions of PCs could be connected. This

Sun Microsystems, Inc.

○ ○ ○

In the late 1970s and early 1980s, more and more buzz was generating around advances in computer technology, and support from the federal government for computing research was at a high point. This was probably because the United States was in an arms-and-technology race with the Soviet Union—and winning. Military applications drove many advancements in computers at this time, but a dedicated group of computer enthusiasts—including researchers at major universities as well as garage-hobbyists, like Apple founders Steve Wozniak and Steve Jobs—started to imagine broader markets for computer hardware and software in commercial industries and for personal use. A few of these far-sighted inventors and investors banded together in 1982 to form Sun Microsystems, Inc., which would quickly rise to become one of the biggest computer companies in the world.

German-born Andy Bechtolsheim was a graduate student at Stanford University working on a computer "workstation" for the Stanford University Network. He met earlier Stanford Business School graduates Scott McNealy and Vinod Khosla, who worked for Daisy Systems and Onyx Systems, respectively; both companies were driving advancements in microchip technology. These three quickly moved to form a computer hardware and software manufacturing company, taking the initials of their alma mater's Stanford University Network. Bill Joy, a Berkeley graduate working on an operating system called Unix for Bell Labs (later AT&T), the dominant telephone company in North America for more than a century, soon joined them. These four secured funding from investors and wasted no time in disrupting and reshaping the computing world.

In its first decade, Sun cashed in on Joy's experience working on Unix by selling affordable workstations (computers for scientific and technical needs) that used the Unix operating system. They later expanded into servers (hardware for storing data). Sun's longest-lasting achievement, however, is probably the invention of the programming language and development platform Java, which brought Sun into new markets for smartphones and other consumer electronics, and which has greater name recognition than Sun itself.

Java lives on, but Sun's success couldn't last. Early investment in Sun was based on the company's quality and reasonably priced products, as well as on its developers' record of remarkable innovation. That was fueled, however, by the "dot-com bubble." In the stock market, a "bubble" occurs when people begin trading stocks or goods in a price range far beyond their real value. "Bubbles" don't deflate, or return to a stable state gradually; they burst when investor interest drops off suddenly, and companies built on inflated trading prices collapse.

The dot-com bubble occurred between 1995 and 2001. Interest in the booming internet was so high, and so unreasonable, that companies could increase the value of their stock simply by adding "e" to the front of their name, or ".com" to the end. The bubble burst in January 2000. Companies merged or declared bankruptcy and disappeared; internet-based companies and technology manufacturers lost over $5 trillion in market value, a free fall that the terrorist attacks of September 11, 2001, only accelerated. Some of the companies that survived, like Amazon, Google, and eBay, were left to dominate fields suddenly cleared of competition.

Sun Microsystems, Inc.
continued

○ ○ ○

Sun *did* recover, but not completely. In the late 1990s, Sun's motto was, "We're the dot in dot com," and this wasn't all bluff: serious, successful companies used Sun products for computing. Shockwaves from the bubble bursting hit Sun and knocked the company from its top spot. It suffered another blow in the Great Recession of 2007 to 2009. Soon there was talk of IBM buying Sun, though this deal never came to pass. After twenty-seven years at the top of the computer industry, Sun shareholders sold the company to Oracle for $5.6 billion. Oracle started deep layoffs, while top engineers soon resigned, and the founders—Bechtolsheim, McNealy, Khoslaall, and Joy—went on to successful careers as investors, inventors, and managers of later startups. All are still active in the computer industry today.

had a huge impact on the way Sun did business. The company started to focus more on interconnectivity as an ultimate goal. Part of the "power" McNealy imagined came from the unlimited sharing of information. If one person invents something and keeps it to herself, that technology will stay at its current level of development until the inventor finds a reason and a way to improve it. But if every new invention was shared instantly, all of its parts and processes shared with all of the innovators in the world, then you can bet that some of those people would find way to improve the invention right away. Because of Scott McNealy's attitude and the attitude of others who shared his beliefs, that's how much of the internet works today. We call this an **open-source** model. Open-source means that the original, or "source," code for something is freely available for people to study and change. When someone invents a new tool or language, they very often share that information with the whole world, through the web, giving others the opportunity to improve on what they've made. This speeds up the rate of technological development; you might even say it speeds up the rate of human history.

Keeping their motto, "The network is the computer," in mind, the FirstPerson researchers, still led by Gosling, started work on a browser like Mosaic that would use the language they had created for their now-abandoned *7 device. They studied different areas of the fast-developing tech industry, traveling to consumer electronics manufacturers in Europe and Asia. They saw these consumer electronics, like CD players, pagers, cell phones, cameras, radios, and even toy helicopters, as being on a "collision course" with the internet. They saw, in other words, the future we now know as the present. They knew that they were creating something powerful, maybe so powerful that it could change the world. But they also knew that something so important needed a better name than Oak.

What's in a Name

"Oak" wouldn't work. It was fine to use as a code word among Sun developers, but another company, Oak Technologies, had trademarked the name, so the Sun employees had to come up with something else before they went public with their new ideas.

Kim Polese, the Oak product manager, gathered the entire team working on the new technology into one room, with a whiteboard in the front. It was January of 1995, and Sun was almost ready to debut their new technology. It would be a good old-fashioned brainstorming session. Polese wanted a name that captured the "essence" of the language and platform—

something "dynamic, revolutionary, lively, fun." The team members started shouting out names, and Polese wrote them on the whiteboard. People in the room that day remember a few of the names suggested: Ruby, Silk, Neon, WRL (for WebRunner Language), DNA, Lyric, Pepper. Gosling recalls the session as "craziness," with at least a dozen people shouting out words and then arguing over the suggestions. They managed to narrow their list down to about a dozen finalists, and sent these to their lawyers. The legal team advised that only Java, DNA, and Silk were safe choices.

One programmer, Arthur Van Hoff, credits another colleague, Chris Warth, as the one who shouted out "Java" first. Warth doesn't remember if he offered the name "Java" or not, but he does admit to having a cup of Peet's Java—the coffee of choice at Sun in those days—in hand at the meeting.

Sometimes used as a synonym for coffee, Java is actually the name of one of the islands that make up Indonesia. Dutch traders brought the coffee plant, native to Ethiopia, from their Indian colonies to Indonesia at the end of the seventeenth century. Within a decade, the Dutch East India Company was shipping the first "Java beans" for sale in Europe. Today, Indonesia is the fourth largest producer of coffee in the world. While beans from other islands are growing in popularity—like the Sumatra, Bali, and Sulawesi

James Gosling

○   ○   ○

Sporting shoulder-length gray hair, a matching beard, and the same pair of spectacles he wore in the 1970s, today James Gosling looks like the Santa Claus of the San Francisco Bay Area. Though Gosling prefers graphic T-shirts to red suits and barbecues to milk and cookies, like Saint Nick his work is almost mythological, and he's admired and adored all across the computer industry.

Born in 1955 in Alberta, Canada, Dr. Gosling is a computer scientist best known for his work on Java. He earned his BSc at the University of Calgary and earned his MS and PhD at Carnegie Mellon University, completing his doctoral dissertation in 1983. Within a year, he was employed as a software developer at Sun Microsystems, Inc., a young and quickly growing company. Between 1984 and 2010, Gosling worked for Sun, where he eventually led the team that created Java. While many researchers and programmers were involved with inventing Java, most credit Gosling as the "father" of the language and platform. Gosling invented Oak, the language that preceded Java, in the early 1990s, and he was a key player who helped shift the attention of Sun developers—and the world at large—toward the internet.

Another technology company, Oracle, bought Sun in 2009, and as usually happens with mergers and buyouts, the culture of the company changed. According to Gosling, he took a pay cut and a demotion and lost many of the freedoms he had enjoyed for twenty-six years at Sun. Within a year, he'd quit the company that he'd helped to change the world.

After taking some time off, Gosling moved to Google, where he was a software engineer. Gosling was far from the first ex-Sun employee to move to Google. Many had come before him, and Google had used Java to create its popular Android phones, which had overtaken the iPhone as the most popular cellular device on the market. However, Oracle was convinced that Google had broken the law in using so much Java code. As owners, they were determined to take Google to court and win a large settlement. Gosling was caught in a difficult position and didn't speak much about the lawsuit during his short time at Google.

After just six months there, he moved to Liquid Robotics, where he is currently Chief Software Architect. Now he makes intelligent robots that collect data from the ocean. Some of his recent projects include improving car safety and working toward safer self-driving cars. He has been a longtime board member of DIRTT, an environmentally conscious interior design and construction company, and he has shared his interest in reforming the American health care system using some of the principles that helped create Java. He still speaks regularly to audiences of Java developers and enthusiasts, and journalists often ask him to speculate about future uses for the language.

No programming
language influenced
smartphones more than
Java—a good name for
our on-the-go culture.

beans—Java remains the most widely recognized name of any coffee-producing island.

Facing pressure from the engineers eager to get their work out into the world, Kim Polese, in charge of marketing, would have made the final decision, after testing the name on friends, colleagues, and family members. No one can know for sure if the language and platform now known as "Java" would have been so successful under a different name, but it is clear that the name "Java" didn't hurt. The name seems to suggest everything its makers hoped it would: "Java" still sounds energetic, hopeful, exotic, swift, jazzy, and hip. Gosling, Warth, and the others probably weren't thinking about the island, about Dutch and Southeast Asian colonial history, or even about the economics of the global coffee trade, but they unwittingly named their soon-to-be break-out, revolutionary brand after another product, the drinkable Java, that had changed the world centuries before. The name fit. Today, Java remains the most popular programming language used, and developers continue to think up new uses for it every day.

The Debut: When the World First Imagined What Java Could Do

The news that Java was going to be demonstrated to the public came as a surprise to James Gosling. His coworker John Gage came into Gosling's office one day in early 1995 and asked to borrow some cables and desktop systems. He said, casually, that he was going to a conference of Hollywood and Silicon Valley big shots, to demonstrate the WebRunner browser the Java team had been working on—secretly. Afraid that their work-in-progress might crash in front of this influential audience, Gosling came along for the ride, as a troubleshooter.

The demonstration started without difficulty, but Gosling noticed that the audience wasn't paying much attention. People weren't very excited about the fact that a new language they didn't understand powered a version of a web browser that looked a lot like a web browser that already existed. Seeing this, Gosling made a series of motions that you, too, have made countless times. He dragged his cursor across the screen to a little 3D graphic of a molecule. Remember, the graphic alone wasn't exciting—developers had already placed images and videos within web pages. But Gosling did something on the screen that no one in the audience

Java powers your smartphone, but it also helps to run massive supercomputers. This property is called scaling.

had ever seen before. He clicked his mouse, and dragged it downward. The molecule moved.

It doesn't seem like much, but that small movement was revolutionary. For the first time ever, users could interact with web pages. Gosling and Gage demonstrated other uses for their language, including an **applet**—or a program that performs a small task—that sorted lines of different lengths. Again, this doesn't seem impressive now, but it demonstrated what would soon become possible with Java.

The old "Green Team" released Java to friends a month later, and then to the entire internet after that, and watched as the downloads climbed into the hundreds, then past ten thousand, then past one million. They took turns dealing with thousands of emails each day. Even bigger news came when the executives of the company Netscape announced that they would start using Java in Navigator, their popular web browser. It was becoming clear then that Java would help to shape the future of the internet.

After that, Java became the most popular computer programming language. Many new languages have debuted since Java's release, and a few other, very different languages compete with it for loyalty from programmers, but Java has been an enormous influence on most languages that have come to follow. Java was hugely influential in the development of smartphones and other technologies, because Java can work across different operating systems, and it can **scale** easily, which means that it can work in small consumer electronics and smartphone apps (like *Pokémon Go*) as well as big things, like supercomputers. More important than any one technical accomplishment, though, is that Java changed the way we think about computers, about our relationship with computers, and about what we can accomplish with them. To understand that, though, you need to know a little bit more about how Java works.

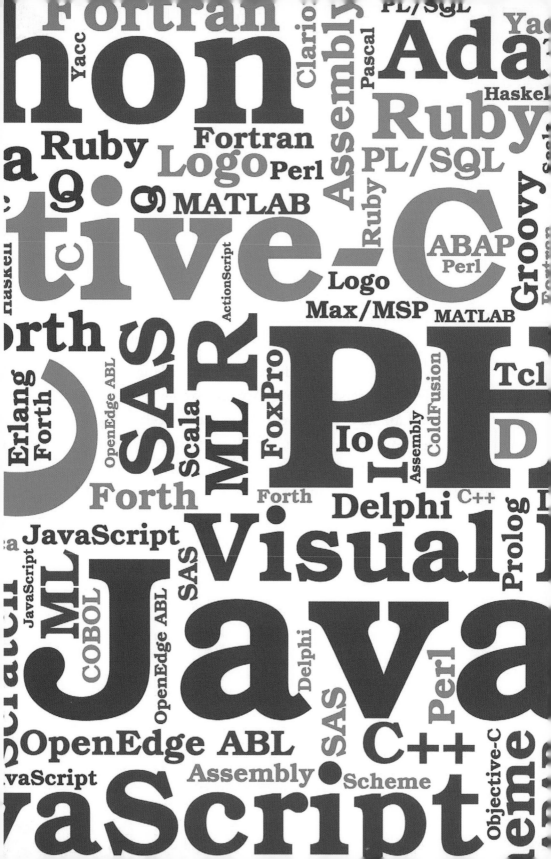

Chapter Two

How It Works

So far we've mostly referred to Java as a language, but to understand how it works—and why it was so revolutionary—we have to understand Java as both a language and a platform. In this chapter, you'll learn the Java basics: what it looks like, what it does, and what makes it unique and effective. We'll explain how something no one speaks can be a language and discuss the features that helped Java revolutionize the computer industry.

Opposite: Every programming language has different features. Choosing a language for a project depends on your goals.

What Is Language?

You can't use Java to ask questions—but you can use it to command. You can't use Java to write poems—but it powers parts of websites like YouTube and SoundCloud, where creative people share their art. Even though it doesn't look like the English you're reading right now, Java is a language.

Your first language was something you learned without realizing it. It was part of your environment. You probably can't remember learning your first language, because it happens so early. Most of us become fluent in our first language without really trying and only later learn the rules. Your parents made noises at you, and your incredibly powerful baby-brain first memorized a few and commanded your little lungs, throat, tongue, and lips to move and make those same noises. At the same time, you started noticing patterns. You didn't know what a "name" was, what it meant to name something or to have a name, but you noticed that people always made the same noise when they looked at you. This was your first step to understanding who and what you are.

If you learn a new language, whether in school or after moving to a new community, the process might be difficult and take a long time, but you're still learning a set of rules that evolved over thousands of years. In spoken languages like English and Spanish and Afrikaans, new words pop up seemingly out of nowhere each year, people regularly break the rules of grammar, and people speaking the same language but in different places on Earth will refer to the same thing with different words. British and American people both speak English, but the British call the back of a car the "boot," while Americans call it the "trunk." The British wear trainers, Canadians wear runners, and Americans wear sneakers: three words that all might be used to refer to the exact same pair of Nikes.

Spoken languages are constantly changing, because real, living people control them by a sort of messy majority rule. That means any user has the potential to change the language. This happens all the time in English. Someone *alive today* was the first to say "Google" (as a verb), "selfie," "bling," "bromance," "hater," "LOL," and "noob." Today, if you use these words, most English speakers will know what you mean—but when we break too many rules or make up too many words, the results can be funny, or they can cause communication to come to a grinding halt.

So-called dead languages, like Latin or Pictish or Ubykh, don't work this way. Because ordinary people (not academics) don't speak these languages, their vocabularies never grow and their grammatical rules will stay the same, as long as anyone remembers them.

Computer programming languages are somewhere in between these two. Programming languages,

Ada Lovelace: the Poet-Programmer

○ ○ ○

Born in 1815 and raised by her mother, an English aristocrat named Annabella Milbanke, Ada Byron, the Countess of Lovelace, would live only thirty-six years and die alone following a painful battle with cancer. In her short life, however, she struggled past the

Ada Lovelace helped spread the earliest computer research.

limited educational opportunities then available to women, earned the love and respect of friends and admirers across the world, and eventually became known as "the first computer programmer."

Ada was the daughter of Lord Byron, one of the most famous of all British poets. Byron left Annabella just two months after Ada was born, to pursue adventures in the Greek War of Independence against the Ottoman Empire. He died there in 1824, when Ada was still a child. Byron was a great traveler and a man of odd habits. Some people found him romantic and inspiring, and others found him scandalous and offensive. Upset with Byron, Annabella tried to influence her daughter Ada away from his poetry—and what she thought was his "madness"—and encouraged the young girl to study math and science instead. Though Ada never knew her father, she developed a lifelong interest in his work. The result of this divided education was an unusual (and powerful) intelligence: Ada's mind was equally suited to mathematical as well as artistic thought.

When Ada was a teenager, she met Charles Babbage, an inventor and mathematician. As the Industrial Revolution picked up steam in the early 1800s, scientists and businesspeople needed workers to produce (and copy) lots of complicated calculations without any errors. Babbage imagined a machine that could do these calculations automatically. He called this the "Difference Engine."

Theory raced ahead of technology. Babbage had imagined a machine with parts too difficult for metalworkers to make at a reasonable cost. Still, conversations with the intelligent and curious Ada spurred him on to further theories and inventions. Babbage was so inspired by Ada's mind that he called her "the Enchantress of Numbers." For her part, Ada was a key figure in popularizing and refining these developments in mathematics and the field that would eventually become computer programming. She translated work by foreign mathematicians into English, and she published extensive and beautifully written notes on the latest thinking in mathematics. Building off Babbage's work, she described how the computer might be automated to do certain complex calculations—really *programs*, like what we can do today with Java and other languages. In these notes and other writings, her mathematical and poetical powers came together. She described complex math and computing in vivid terms anyone could understand. Perhaps because her approach to the field was, as she called it, "poetical science," she was able to imagine the potential for the computer beyond what anyone else at the time could see.

like Java, C, and HTML, are "living," because real people use them and could even end up changing them. Unlike spoken languages, however, computer-programming languages have "owners": the rules of Java only change when Oracle's programmers decide to change them. If you don't like the rules, you can hope this happens—or, as many programmers have done, you can make up your own, new language.

Understanding Java Syntax

At the most basic level, all languages work the same way. Every language has "packets" of information. For most languages, we call the smallest packets "letters" and bigger packets "words." For example, the letter "D" contains information: if you know the letter, you know what it's supposed to sound like when it's spoken as a part of a word. You can probably list a hundred words right now that begin with the letter "D." When you put these packets together, they can mean something much more than just a sound. For example, if you put the letters D-O-G together, you've made the word *dog*, and that packet carries a lot of information. Just seeing the word *dog* in print probably puts an image in your mind. You might think of dachshunds or retrievers, bulldogs, or poodles. You feel love or affection thinking of your own pet or a friend or neighbor's pet. You might remember fear, thinking of the time you saw an angry dog, or you might feel sadness, thinking of a dog that died. All this—all these feelings and images—are only possible because you know what the shapes D, O, and G mean when they're placed together.

All languages also have a **syntax**, or a set of rules about how those packets of information can be put together, and how their arrangement can carry much more meaning than any of the packets could on their own. You can say the word "dog" to another English speaker and trust that he or she understands what you mean. But if you want to say something *about* a dog, you need more words, and that could quickly get confusing if you didn't share a set of rules about how to use those words. Grammar lets us express our deepest feelings, give more complicated instructions, and turn our dreams of how the world might be into reality by sharing those dreams with other people.

Math is a language, too. It has packets of information—numbers, as well as symbols like plus and minus signs, decimals, and parentheses—and the syntax of math is the set of rules that allows us to interpret these signs, or packets of information, when they're arranged in complex patterns.

Like any other language—like English, German, or mathematics—Java also has packets of information and a syntax allowing us to arrange and interpret them. In fact, it's one of the easier programming languages to learn, once you understand some of its basic features.

Understanding Objects

The way Java handled information and commands was revolutionary. Unlike other languages built around commands, instructions to a computer to "do this" or "do that," Java is an **object-oriented** language. Instead of actions, **objects** are at the center of everything in Java.

So, what are objects? "Object" is a single word that can mean many things. In fact, we can often use it interchangeably with "thing." In English, we use the word "object" to refer to anything that has physical properties—in other words, anything we can sense. If you can touch, taste, smell, hear, and see something, it might be an object. Often, we use the word when we don't have a better, more specific word ready. For example, you might call something strange shooting across the night sky a "UFO" (Unidentified Flying Object).

In computer programming, an object is a package of data and operations, or actions that happen to that data. Packaging data in this way allows programmers to work on different parts of their program separately—a great help when working with large, complicated projects. The first object-oriented language was called

Simula, invented in 1967, but Java was the first object-oriented language widely used.

Programmers say that objects have **states**, or characteristics, and **behaviors**, or things the object can do or that can happen to the object. To understand this, it might help to think of real-world objects. You could say that a fish is an object. Every fish has "states" (characteristics): it has a name, a shape, and a color. The fish also has behaviors: it can swim with its fins; it can use its gills to take oxygen from the water; it can eat and be eaten. There are infinite objects in the universe, with infinite states and behaviors. This is also true of Java.

And just as we love to classify things in the real world—organizing fish by species, family, and native environments—we also put Java objects into a **class**, or a general blueprint for creating individual objects. Classes say which states and behaviors objects within the class can have. When you finish writing a new program, you save it as a new class.

Finally, a programmer can express an object's behaviors through a **method**, a part of the code that says what will happen to an object, or how objects will interact with each other. The primary method in a class is called a **main**.

Code Structure and Syntax

As you might have guessed already, objects make programming complex tasks much easier. Objects let programmers focus on individual pieces of their code one at a time, before putting the objects together.

As stated in the previous section, classes are like blueprints for creating objects, which means before you make an object, you need a class. Let's say your dog ripped out the title page of this book. Because you want to fix the book and test out your programming skills at the same time, you decide to write a program that will print out a new title page for the book. (Don't worry about how the program connects to your printer. Check the back of this book for more resources that will teach you about that.) You'd start by writing something like this:

```
public class TitlePagePrinterApp {
```

"Public" means anyone can see your app. "Class" signals that the name of your app will follow: we named this app "TitlePagePrinterApp." Finally, the curly bracket, { , signals the opening of the class. Basically, all the code that *does* stuff comes after the curly bracket. So, once you add a method (to make your program *do* something) it could look like this:

```
public class TitlePagePrinterApp {
    public static void main (String[] args) {
        System.out.print ("The Power of Java");
    }
}
```

Don't worry about knowing what every single word or character here does. Beneath the opening line of your TitlePagePrinterApp you've added the main method, which contains a statement about what your app will do. The statement is on the third line:

```
System.out.print ("The Power of Java");
```

In this case, you've told your app to print the characters "The Power of Java." This is called a string. In Java, a string is just a packet of information, or data. The data is what you want to print: the title of this book. Every statement ends with a semicolon (;). The first curly bracket closes the main method, and the second curly bracket closes the class, TitlePagePrinterApp.

By this point you've learned a lot about Java, and you also feel like playing a bit of a prank on your librarian, or the next person to pick up this book. So, you make your code a little more advanced:

```
public class TitlePagePrinterApp {
    public static void main (String[] args) {
        System.out.println ("The Power of Java");
        System.out.println ("by Stella Lopez");
    }
}
```

Now, your program prints a title page with two lines: "The Power of Java" above your name (which probably isn't Stella Lopez—you could make your program write anything here). You've added "ln" to "print" in each statement to put the statements on separate lines. If you wanted to, you could reproduce the *entire book* this way, typing whole chapters into different statements.

Object-Oriented: Coding Beyond the "Main"

The code you just wrote, though, doesn't take advantage of Java's power to work with objects. To really understand the power of Java, you'd have to write code with multiple classes creating multiple objects that can interact with each other.

If you've ever played Tetris, thinking about this game could help you understand objects in Java. In this game, squares clumped together form different shapes: one is a bigger square, one is a straight line, one looks like an L, one looks like an uppercase T, one looks like a plus sign, and one makes a zigzag. These fall from the top of the screen to the bottom of the screen, and players can rotate them as they fall, trying to stack the pieces to make straight, horizontal lines. Horizontal lines crossing the entire screen will disappear, but if there are gaps, the pieces in a line stay put. The pieces keep falling and stacking, and if the pile reaches the top of the screen, the player loses.

Java would be an excellent tool for making a game like Tetris. In fact, many people already have made imitations of Tetris using Java. With a little work, you could, too. You might start by making a class called "blocks." Remember that a class is like a blueprint for making different objects. From your class, blocks, you could make all the objects you need to play the game: the square piece, the straight piece, the T piece, the L piece, the plus sign piece, and the zigzag piece. Like all objects in Java, each would have states and behaviors. The states could be their sizes and colors. The behaviors could be the different speeds at which they fall, and the ways players could rotate them in the "air." You'd also have to write a method (a specific behavior) about how the pieces could interact. In this case, you'd write a method making the pieces disappear whenever the player

Java works by making easily replicable objects,
which makes it perfect for games like Tetris.

creates an unbroken horizontal line of blocks along
the bottom of the screen. This program would be a
lot longer than your program to print a new title page
for this book. However, writing it in Java would be
much easier than in another language, especially a
language that isn't object-oriented.

Your Tetris program demonstrates the last thing
you need to know (for now!) about objects in Java.
Your program actually uses all three types of methods
possible in Java:

- Statements: Your program *does something*.
  Statements only happen once, and
  happen automatically. For example, a
  statement could do something as simple

as start the game as a player opens the program. If you wanted to get fancier, you could add a statement to present a title screen. This code would look pretty similar to your "TitlePagePrinterApp" code.

- Loops: Loops are methods that repeat themselves … over and over and over, until the program stops running. In your Tetris game, you'd use a "loop" method for the falling blocks. You want these blocks to keep falling, to challenge the player.

- Branching: This method is "triggered." It happens *if*: if something else happens, or under a certain set of conditions. This is the type of method you would use to make the blocks disappear. This doesn't happen automatically, and it doesn't loop without stopping. Pieces only disappear under a certain condition: *if* the player lines up a row of squares. (You could also write a branching method to make a big "YOU LOSE" sign pop up, triggered by the blocks reaching the top of the screen.)

Beyond Language: Compiler, Platform, and Machine

Remember that the other great promise of Java, besides the "object-oriented" approach, is **portability.** That means you can write it on any platform, and it can run on any other platform. Imagine if a spoken language worked this way. Imagine that you were standing in front of the entire United Nations with a speech to deliver. You wrote the speech in English, but as soon as the words left your lips, hundreds of other people could understand your speech in their own languages— Spanish, Hindi, Arabic, Afrikaans, Mandarin, and so on—without the aid of a real-time translator. Imagine speaking in English and not having any doubt that all other people in the world could understand you, no matter what language they chose to speak. This would be an amazing power (and a lot of translators would need to find new jobs).

Java works this way because of something called the **compiler**. The Java compiler is a program that takes Java source code and transforms it into another programming language. In this case, we're talking about assembly language, which is specific to different machines. So, a Windows computer, an Apple computer, a Linux computer, and an Android phone will each have its own assembly language; so will a

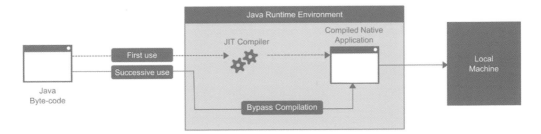

The Java Virtual Machine is the technology behind the Java's promise to "Write Once, Run Anywhere."

digital watch, a radio/alarm clock, and a TV. The Java compiler can take the plain text of your program (like the "TitlePagePrinterApp" we made earlier) and "compile" it into a .class file written in **bytecode**. All you really need to know about bytecode is that you couldn't "read" it, and that it's not native to any machine or platform.

Instead, this bytecode goes to the **Java Virtual Machine (JVM)**, which is like a virtual computer. This JVM can work on *any* platform or machine, using the Java Application Programming Interface (**API**). Because an API is a set of instructions that allow a platform to run a program, with the help of the Java API, the JVM can run your code on any platform. As you can imagine, the possibilities of such a "portable" language are limitless.

The Wave Glider

○ ○ ○

Owned by the company Boeing, which is best known for its airplanes, Liquid Robotics makes and sells something called the Wave Glider, a robot that gathers data from the ocean. Without a pilot, the Wave Glider can float and function on its own for over a year, powered by the energy of the sun, the waves, and—you guessed it—Java.

James Gosling, the "father of Java," joined Liquid Robotics as Chief Software Engineer in 2011. Their Wave Glider software uses the Java programming language. It's not surprising that he ended up here: Gosling always had an interest in "cool toys." During the late 1990s and early 2000s at Sun, Gosling became known for giving fun conference presentations on robots and other devices that did exciting things with Java. This was a small part of his job at Sun (later Oracle), but his interest in "toys" might have led him to his current job programming ocean robots.

The Wave Glider has two parts. There is a platform that floats on the surface of the water, gathering energy through solar panels. Suspended below, a "submarine" uses movable wings to take the energy of the waves and propel itself forward.

Gathering data from the ocean has always been difficult. There's just so much of it—so much ocean and so much data. Research has been expensive and full of dangers. The Wave Glider, however, can collect all sorts of information and upload it immediately to cloud storage, so researchers can get to it without ever checking in on the robot in person. It can help environmentalists gather data on weather and wave patterns and even sonic information about animal migration. Militaries and other government operations can use it to patrol borders, detect threats, and combat piracy and smuggling. It can even help energy companies explore natural resources and reduce risk to human employees. The robot can "swim" on its own for a year or more, avoiding obstacles like ships on its own (probably using a series of "branching" methods in its Java code). Some Wave Gliders have survived hurricanes and shark attacks. Best of all, the Wave Glider requires no refueling and no manpower, and it doesn't pollute the atmosphere in any way. It's so efficient that most of the energy it takes from the sun goes toward its powerful computers. This technology should have applications beyond Earth, too: if we ever discover another planet covered in liquid, scientists would probably use a version of the Wave Glider to explore it.

According to Gosling, one of Java's most powerful applications is in **artificial intelligence (AI)**. This means any computer that can make some decisions on its own and can "teach," or improve, itself. The Wave Glider is one example. While writing the software, Gosling included an instruction for the gliders: basically, "don't be afraid of ships." Now captains are afraid of crashing into gliders, until they see the "smart" robots change course and avoid the collision on their own. This is very easy to do in Java, Gosling says, and would be much harder in other languages. On top of that, the glider is based on one of the core beliefs and goals of the old Green Team: it can communicate the information it gathers across any platform.

<Chapter Three/>

Strengths and Weaknesses

I t's clear that Java is a pretty powerful tool. You can use it to make websites appealing, fun, and interactive. You can use it to design cool video games. And because of the compiler and Java Virtual Machine, you can easily port your Java program between different devices.

Remember, though, that Java isn't the only programming language, and it isn't the "best." There can't be a "best" programming language, just like there couldn't be a "best" spoken, human language. Each one is beautiful and fascinating in its own way. Each allows

Opposite: The best way to understand the strengths and weaknesses of a computer language is to jump in and start coding.

The campus of Bell Laboratories, where Dennis Ritchie got his start.

for different types of expressions or applications. In fact, computer-programming languages are most like spoken human languages in this way. They often accomplish the most when people use different languages together. In this chapter, you'll learn more about how Java compares to other languages: what its strengths and weaknesses are, and how you might use it along with other languages to do things none could accomplish on their own.

Growing Java from an Oak Tree, and an Oak Tree from a "C"

Recall that James Gosling worked on an earlier version of the Java language, before the rest of his team picked a name. He called this language Oak. Even Oak didn't appear out of nowhere, though. It grew from the seed of C.

Or, rather, it grew from the frustration Gosling and others felt using the much-older programming languages C and C++. C had been around since the early 1970s. C++ appeared in 1983. You might remember that computers "speak" to themselves in machine language, the binary code of ones and zeroes. Because it isn't easy to make a computer do anything writing in machine language, developers built other languages on top and called these assembly languages. Assembly languages were still a little clumsy, though, so an engineer named Dennis Ritchie working at Bell Labs (a hundred-year-old communications monopoly that became AT&T) designed C as an easier-to-use language that bypassed the assembly languages and mapped right onto machine language.

Java would not have been possible without Dennis Ritchie's language called C.

C was a great leap forward, and it remains one of the most popular languages developers use today. But it has many downsides, and this frustrated the developers pushing at the frontiers of what computers could do. C's shortcomings included the following:

- Function Orientation: Instead of working around objects that a developer could isolate and produce easily from the "blueprint" of a class, C was built around functions, or individual commands that lack blueprints and are harder to work on in isolation.
- Poor Portability: Though Ritchie designed C to work across different platforms, this was easier imagined than done. A skilled programmer would have to take on the time-consuming job of recompiling (and sometimes rewriting) code for each new platform.
- Inefficient Use of Memory: C had no built-in way of making a program automatically manage memory. This meant complicated programs could slow down.

In short, then, C was an advancement, but as programmers found they had more complicated projects and bigger dreams, C seemed too slow, too inefficient, too time-consuming to write, and not adaptive enough. This doesn't mean that C is useless—engineers still prefer C for **embedded systems**, computers inside things like stop lights and thermostats—but new uses for computers called for new languages.

Bjarne Stoustrup, an engineer, fixed the "object" problem in 1983 by introducing C++. This offered a sleeker, more efficient, and easier-to-use version of C, by making the language object-oriented.

The Object-Oriented Approach

As you've already learned, object-oriented programming began as a way to tackle more complex projects more easily. It does this in two ways. First, it "packages" data and the operations on data (things that a program "does" to data) into objects. It then arranges these objects into classes based on what's in them and what they do. Finally, it hides most of these details from public users.

Imagine that you're building a house. You have the plot of land picked and the four corners marked with stakes. But all the stuff that you'll need to build the house—bricks, boards, nails, shingles, pipes, wires, cement blocks, and window panes—is just sitting in a pile next to your building site. And mixed in with these basics, you also have rolls of wallpaper, bits of wood and stuffing for furniture, kitchen appliances, clothes, picture frames, lightbulbs, cookie jars, and paintings.

If you tried to dive right in and start building the house, you'd be frustrated pretty quickly. This is how computer programmers were feeling. Earlier programmers had been doing simpler things—the way building a chair is simpler than building a house. If you're just building a chair, you can look at your pile of materials, ignore the cookie jar and everything else you don't need and build the chair without too much work. But if you're building a house, you might have the bright idea to organize your materials first. You could put all your bricks in one pile and all your shingles in another. You could place all the materials you would need to make the frame of the house near each other, and you could put all your plumbing materials somewhere else. This is the same impulse that led to object-oriented programming: organization.

C++ and Java: an Object-Oriented Comparison

The first object-oriented language was Simula, released in 1967. Stoustrup used the object-oriented approach to improve C with C++ in 1983, but even C++ had its shortcomings. Linus Torvalds, the developer of the Linux operating system, calls C++ a "horrible" language (maybe a little unfairly). Today, most Windows and Adobe programs (like Word and Photoshop) are written in C++, as are most video games for systems like Xbox and PlayStation. However, while C++ may be easy to learn, its complexity makes it difficult to master. It's a "wordy," or dense language. Code in C++ tends to be longer than comparable code in Java, and even the error messages can be long and confusing. It also compiles slowly, and it doesn't use memory efficiently.

James Gosling and his team designed Java to fix a lot of these problems. Java code is shorter and sleeker; it compiles quickly; and it introduced something called **garbage collection**, a memory-management tool that reclaims memory from objects or functions that the program isn't using anymore. It's hard to deny that Java is the most widely used and one of the most successful object-oriented languages.

Language Barriers and Interoperability

Imagine that you, an English speaker, were to meet someone who spoke only Russian. Even though English and Russian share some basic structures, you probably wouldn't get very far with one speaking in English and the other responding in Russian. Programming languages work the same way. Java, C++, Python, and other languages can't "speak" directly to each other. At least, they can't speak to each other without some kind of bridge. However, the demands of computing today mean languages have to work together all the time. This is called **interoperability**: the ability of programming languages to interact and operate on the same data.

Some languages, like Groovy, Clojure, and Scala, were built to run on the Java Virtual Machine and can interact with anything in a Java library (a collection of objects or other data structures). Whole new languages sometimes result from attempts to map existing languages onto each other—as is the case with Jython, an attempt to port the language Python for the Java Virtual Machine. Any web page you visit will involve even more languages, usually some combination

Tim Berners-Lee invented the internet so that average citizens could share information and ideas.

of HTML (the first language Tim Berners-Lee created to write web pages) and JavaScript (a language for making web pages interactive, not possible with HTML alone). More complicated web pages might use **plug-ins**, or applets that make sites do more "stuff." Pop-up advertisements, embedded videos, comment boxes, and search functions are all plug-ins. Plug-ins allow developers to write applications in languages like Java or PHP and run them on web pages written in HTML and JavaScript.

All these examples of interoperability work because the languages we use to program can all compile to simpler codes, which can then translate to machine language. Imagine that your new Russian friend has come to help you build your house. You have neatly arranged your materials into piles, but you call a hammer a hammer, and your Russian friend calls it a *molot*. When you want something, you say, "Hand me …" and your Russian friend says, "*Day mne …*" You might think of what needs to be done in English, but you'd have to translate these commands into something simpler, like hand gestures. Your Russian friend would interpret the gestures into her own language—Russian—before carrying out the action (through the "machine language" of messages between the brain and the body parts). Programming languages interact like this—though much more efficiently!

Write Once, Run Anywhere

In chapter 2 you learned more about the Java compiler and the promise of portability. Java developers were supposed to be able to write programs once, on one platform, and run them *anywhere*. A developer could write a source code for a program, then compile it into

Java bytecode. Any operating system equipped with the Java Virtual Machine could then open and run that file in a language that the platform (whether a Windows or an Apple computer, an iPad, or a Google Pixel smartphone) could "understand."

This built on an earlier coding language, Pascal, dating back to the 1970s. Researchers at the University of California at San Diego found that they and their students needed a common coding language that would work on the different microcomputers across campus, so they invented the Pascal language and the P-system on which it ran. Though the company IBM supported Pascal, the P-system was expensive and reviewers didn't love the results. However, it was one of the first attempts to use a virtual machine. James Gosling worked with Pascal while a graduate student at Carnegie Mellon, and this experience influenced the direction he would take with Java years later.

"Write once, run anywhere," turned out to be a good catchphrase. The Sun marketing team soon started using the shorthand WORA. The catch, of course, is that to run a Java program, an operating system needs to be equipped with the Java Virtual Machine. Java became so popular so quickly, though, that installation of JVM or a Java interpreter became an industry standard for most systems.

Grace Under Pressure: Scaling with Java

Java can run anything from programmable toasters to supercomputers to "smartcards" (like contactless credit and debit cards). Especially since the rise of smartphones, developers have used Java to create apps that become overnight sensations. No matter the language a developer used to write them, useful or innovative apps are often overwhelmed with downloads and usage, crashing servers, revealing bugs, and slowing performance. That leaves a poor impression on users who might be on the fence about downloading the app or switching to a competitor. Though performance depends on the programmer's skill, Java is a particularly useful language for designing apps and software to scale, or "grow," gracefully.

Scalability is one way of measuring the performance of a computer, server, or software program under intense pressure from many users trying to perform many tasks at the same time—so scalability doesn't matter much for that programmable toaster, but it's very important for apps and video games. As far as Java is concerned, a program is highly scalable if it can continue to perform quickly and without crashing as usage continues to increase. The higher the threshold—the point at which a program has too many

NASA's World Wind: an Interoperability Study

○ ○ ○

NASA's World Wind is a virtual globe, sort of like Google Earth, but customizable, and loaded up with an extraordinary amount of data from NASA's satellites and other equipment on Earth and in space.

With World Wind, users can explore the Earth—and even Mars, Venus, Jupiter, and several moons—in real-time, watching as the sun's light recedes and cities brighten in the night. Mountains and other topographical features display in 3D, and with plug-ins you can even overlay pinpoints that link to Wikipedia articles, on things like the Great Wall of China or the Marianas Trench.

These plug-ins call on a host of programming languages, like C#, J#, and VB. In the beginning, World Wind was only available on Microsoft operating systems, but NASA scientists wanted to bring it to everyone through the web, which meant it would have to run through a browser's HTML and work on any operating system. Bringing such a powerful program to absolutely any user—even users of smartphones and tablets—would be a huge challenge for interoperability, so NASA programmers used Java to make it happen.

World Wind Java, released in 2017, made the entire World Wind program a Java applet capable of running (through HTML) on a web page on any operating system, still including all the plug-ins in other languages, and still calling on data from hundreds of NASA projects collected with software built with countless other programming languages.

and communication across the barriers of the early internet. Even as a teenager in the 1960s and 1970s, he worked on computer projects that tried to bridge gaps between platforms, systems, and languages. His greatest achievement in this was inventing Java, which took that paradigm—a belief in acting and communicating across great human and machine divides—and brought it to a bigger audience: first hundreds of developers, and then thousands, and then millions, and then to the billions of people who use Java without thinking about it.

One example of this "cross-platform paradigm" in action was the invention of **Virtual Network Computing**, or **VNC**. In the late 1980s, most computing was done on desktops. However, the possibilities, especially graphical possibilities, of computing, created a demand for scientists and businesspeople to use computers to deliver visual presentations in different locations. Today we have cloud storage services like OneDrive, Dropbox, and Google Drive, but back then, computer users were far more limited, and data sharing was not a quick or easy affair. Presenters would have limited options for traveling with computer files. They could transfer files to a floppy disk and hope that it would run on another computer, but if they needed to continue working on a project as they traveled, they couldn't store their entire computing environment (everything you'd find on a desktop hard drive) on a floppy disk, and laptops were bulky, heavy, expensive, and fragile.

Researchers at Cambridge came up with a solution. It was one of the first great new applications of Java, and it very much fit the Java paradigm. Virtual Network Computing allows a user on one computer to access the display of another computer—from anywhere in the world. That means that a traveler could use a hotel computer (these were more common in the late 1980s and 1990s) and sign in to a VNC using any Java-capable web browser. The hotel computer screen would display the screen of the computer back at her home or office. She could continue working on the presentation there. The next day, she could use another computer to access that same home or office computer and deliver the presentation to an audience. VNC isn't limited to simple tasks like presenting slides or papers, either: with VNC, you can remotely perform almost any task that you'd do sitting in front of your own computer. That made it useful for remote technical support and administration. If something goes wrong with your computer and you have VNC set up, a more experienced user can fix your problems from his or her own computer. Because the Cambridge team wrote VNC with Java, it works across platforms: a Mac user could remotely access a Windows desktop, and so on. And VNC isn't limited to display-based platforms. From any VNC-capable computer, you could also access consumer electronics like programmable microwaves, lights, entertainment systems, and home security.

Developments like this, growing out of the Java commitment to access and portability, drove further advances in software, apps, and other technologies that ease communication and collaboration.

Write Once, Debug Everywhere: Cross-Platform Promises and Problems

The Java vision of true, seamless, cross-platform development undeniably helped to expand access to the internet and to computing in the 1990s, but it didn't always live up to the WORA promise. Although the Java compiler does allow a developer to write one program that will work on any platform with a JVM, there are still small differences in the way platforms run programs. Even the compiler and the JVM cannot account for all of these variations. The slight differences between the way a program runs on a Mac versus a PC don't usually matter much. Sometimes, though, they lead to problems, which programmers call **bugs**. In computer programming, a bug is an error that causes the program to fail or work in some way other than what the developer intended. Bugs can be harmless, they can

Java and Objective-C: Developing Apps for Android and iOS

○ ○ ○

In 1998, the telecommunications company Motorola signed a licensing agreement to use Java in its cellular devices. This was the beginning of Java's domination of the smartphone industry. When developers for Android—the preferred operating system for around 80 percent of the smartphone market—wrote their operating system in Java, Java's dominance was complete.

Smartphone manufacturers Apple and Android have been locked in an expensive legal battle. At its heart is the Java programming language.

The biggest competitor of Android devices, currently, is the iPhone. Apple developers created the iPhone OS, and all iPhone apps use Objective-C, a language built on top of and compatible with the older C, but including elements from the object-oriented language Smalltalk.

Objective-C and Java are quite different, but most Android or iPhone users don't know or care. No matter which brand they prefer, all smartphone users want the same tools and apps—and with a few exceptions, they get them. Apple developers have to replicate accomplishments from Android—and vice versa—while third-party developers have to build their apps in both languages.

If you take almost any app available on both Android and Apple devices—like Scanvine, which collects trending news stories, or Shazam, which uses the built-in microphone to identify music playing near the user—differences on the user-end are negligible. In most cases, both will do the job equally well. The difference is on the back end.

In a 2015 study, an app development company named Infinum studied its own apps and found that coding for Android (in Java) required 38 percent more lines of code, took 28 percent more time to complete, and was therefore significantly more expensive than writing code for iPhone (in Objective-C). While time and expense are a downside, longer code can actually make for better performance, though it takes longer to debug and maintain.

be irritating, or they can be disastrous—causing whole systems to crash, or destroying data, for example.

Because of these subtle differences in the way Java programs behave on different platforms, Java developers found themselves writing programs once ... and then debugging them several times across different platforms. This led to a tongue-in-cheek take on the Java promise: in practice, many Java programmers felt they had to "Write Once, Debug Everywhere."

Other Limitations of the Java Language and JVM

As recently as 2013, one *Forbes* magazine writer estimated that "Just about every electronic device conceivable uses some amount of Java programming." This is a good thing. A big community of users keeps

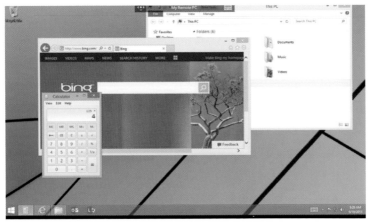

Java's potential for remote computing is a boon for business people traveling for work. However, there have been JVM security concerns.

a computer programming language healthy and always improving. But it also means that structural flaws can cause wide-reaching damage.

In that same year, the US Department of Homeland Security uncovered a serious security flaw in all versions of Java that then existed. It seemed that hackers might be able to manipulate a computer remotely using Java apps—doing things like activating a laptop's camera. Oracle, which then controlled Java, was quick to release an update fixing the security problem, but the stir over the issue was an important reminder about the limitations of any language, and of Java in particular.

As discussed above, even though Java is so widely used, and dominates the smartphone app development community today, many of the major players in software—like Microsoft, Apple, and Adobe—use mostly C++ to build their powerful program suites, while e-merchants like Amazon use it for their large-scale business operations. The entire video game industry also relies on C++, because it has a massive library, allows for complete control, and compiles directly to assembly language (unlike Java, which uses the JVM as a go-between). Meanwhile, embedded systems—computer systems that serve specific purposes inside larger mechanical or electronic systems, like hybrid cars or traffic lights—often use C, because its graceful syntax makes its lines relatively short, and because it doesn't use too much memory.

<Chapter Four/>

Getting Started

In the case of *Pokémon Go*, millions of players and trillions of digital Pokémon had generated Nintendo $1 billion within a few months. All the battles, and most of the phones that players were using, ran on Java. Now you know how that works, and how Java made a phenomenon like *Pokémon Go* possible.

But there was an even bigger "battle" going on the summer the game was released, and it had relatively little to do with collectible cartoon monsters. It *did* involve that popular game, but it also (potentially) involved animations for Hollywood movies, the

Opposite: Java lets us share our great ideas, through texts and emails. But some great ideas might be better expressed in Java itself.

checkout computers at some of your favorite stores, and even the onboard computers of the NASA Mars exploration rovers. More than $9 billion was at stake, along with the future of the smartphone industry and the very culture of computer programming. The issue is one that could matter very much to you, and to anyone considering a career in computers. The whole programming world watched and wondered: *Will the Java language always be free for anyone to use?*

Battle Over Java, and the Smartphone Wars

To understand the "smartphone wars" and what these have to do with computer programming in general,

Oracle CEO Larry Ellison oversaw the purchase of Sun Microsystems—and the rights to Java—in 2009.

we have to look a little more closely at the Oracle purchase of Sun Microsystems, Inc.

Riding on strong hardware sales and the runaway success of Java, Sun became more and more devoted to the principles of open-source technology that had helped to shape its beginnings. In 1999, Sun bought the rights to software that competed with Microsoft's Office Suite (Word, Excel, PowerPoint, and so on), and released this for free. Then, the dot-com bubble burst shortly after. As Sun was a major player, the bubble bursting hit them hard, but not hard enough to crush them. The company returned to health, but it would never return to its old position of dominance; Microsoft, Apple, and Google were the new major players.

But Sun hung on, in large part due to Java, its enduring popularity, and its growing role in mobile phone technology. In 2005, Sun released over 1,600 patents to the public, and in 2006, the company made Java open source. This left control over Java in Sun's hands, but anyone could see the source code, use it, and adapt it. The company continued to enjoy strong sales and growth.

Everything changed with the start of the Great Recession in December 2007. As the global economy slowed, stock prices dropped—again. This time, the bubble wasn't confined to the tech industry.

Consumers started spending less, and many companies like Sun suffered. Rumors of Sun mergers and buyouts circulated in business magazines and websites. Then, in April of 2009, another technology company called Oracle stepped in and bought Sun Microsystems, Inc. for around $7.4 billion.

Not surprisingly, the Oracle executives, led by founder and then-CEO Larry Ellison, had some different ideas about how to do business. According to James Gosling, Oracle executives were excited early on about the prospect of making even more than they'd spent to buy Sun, in a lawsuit against one of the most popular brands in the world: Google.

In September of 2008, Google had released Android, an operating system primarily for touchscreen devices like smartphones and tablets. A small team of developers, led by Andy Rubin, started Android, Inc. in 2003, and Google had bought the company for $50 million two years later, before the system was ready to show the public, bringing the founders along as employees to finish the job. While the core of Android was written in C, its **user interface** (the way users interact with the system) was all Java. This was exactly the kind of use that had led the Sun executives to make Java open source: a powerful innovation from small-time, startup developers. But Google was no small-time startup, and it would soon be making massive profits off code largely lifted—without payment—from Sun.

The iPhone in Korea

While Android was still new on the market, two bigger smartphone producers were gearing up for legal battle on a global scale. In 2010, the Korean company Samsung released the Galaxy S, a phone

Your preference in smartphones might be based on the way a phone looks and responds. No matter the phone, these characteristics depend on Java.

that looked and worked a lot like the Apple iPhone, then the smartphone of choice for many users. After early talks failed, Apple sued Samsung for copyright infringement. After two years, several suits and countersuits, and millions in legal fees, two US juries found that Samsung executives and developers had intentionally stolen parts of the iPhone's technology and design, and demanded that Samsung pay Apple $400 million in damages. Other courts in other countries ruled that both companies had violated each other's patents, and still other courts ruled that neither violated any patents.

The fighting didn't stop in 2012. In December 2016, the US Supreme Court unanimously reversed the earlier decision (and the $400 million award) and sent the case back to a lower court for further legal wrangling. In the meantime, smartphones quite literally took over global culture. As the amount of money involved in the industry grew, the Samsung-Apple battle sucked in nearly every other major smartphone manufacturer and developer, including Microsoft, LG, Nokia, and Sony, all involved in a complicated crosshatch of patent copyright lawsuits. The stakes rose, according to one commentator in the British newspaper the *Guardian*, because of just how many people have a smartphone. In the early days of the technology, most smartphone sales went to people who'd never had one of the devices before. Now, most sales are to people who already have a smartphone. That means for any manufacturer to grow, it has to take a customer away from a competitor. At the same time, the rate of advancement in smartphone technology has slowed.

A Cold Coffee Date: Oracle and Google Fight Over Java

And, of course, one of the companies now at the center of the smartphone wars is Google. Google turned the (Java-based) Android OS into a success—and a target—in part because it's open source, unlike the iPhone OS in Apple's iron grip, but also because manufacturers (including Samsung!) have been able to produce Android phones more cheaply than iPhones.

According to James Gosling, Sun executives had considered suing Google over its use of Java code in the Android system before the Oracle buyout. Scott McNealy and others reasoned that Google *had* violated patents, but the company executives didn't want to sue. Google's use of the lines of code, Gosling said, had a mostly positive impact on the community of Java users and programmers. Suing Google would cost time and money—and it could also be bad for the company's image, because of Google's worldwide popularity.

Oracle bought Sun in April 2009; by August 2010, the company had joined the "smartphone wars," suing Google for patent and copyright infringement, seeking a staggering $9 billion for lost revenues. Google claimed that their adoption of Java code fell under **fair use**—basically, this allows individuals and companies to use copyrighted material in certain circumstances without seeking permission. Google claimed that it could use Java because Java had always been open source—the code had been available to the public from the beginning. A jury voted in Google's favor in late May 2016, but Oracle's lawyers have signaled that they will appeal the ruling.

The future of the Android system, and the freedom of developers to use already-existing code to create new programs, might change, but according to Gosling, at least, Java is "safe," and will always be free for the public to use and to modify. Java is "bigger," he says, than any one developer, application, or even industry.

Java in the Programming Marketplace Today

According to the TIOBE Index, which for two decades has tracked developers' interest in and use of different programming languages, Gosling is right. Java has

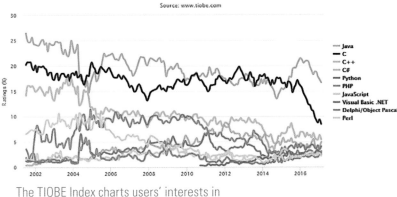

TIOBE Programming Community Index
Source: www.tiobe.com

The TIOBE Index charts users' interests in different computer languages over time.

led the pack—by a wide margin—at least since 2001. At its peak, Java accounted for over 26 percent of all programming. In the time since then, developers have invented many new languages. Now Java accounts for a little over 16.4 percent of all programming; C follows at 7.7 percent, and C++ at 5.1 percent.

Java's popularity began to decline and even fell below C following the Oracle takeover, in part because of new, competing languages, but also, according to TIOBE managing director Paul Jansen, because of the way developers perceived Java under Oracle. The company seemed to be spending more time on things like its lawsuit against Google, and less on maintaining, promoting, and pushing the Java language. Original Java developers (like Gosling) left and started promoting other languages, while Oracle developers didn't do much

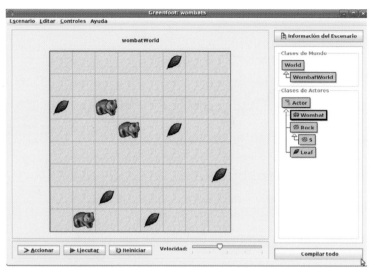

You can learn how to use Java with a free integrated development environment (IDE) like Greenfoot.

to keep Java fresh, or respond to everyday programmers' concerns, according to one *Wired* magazine analysis.

Java's dip was short-lived, as was C's return to prominence. C, not very well-suited to mobile web and app development, has plummeted, while Java, an excellent language for that kind of work, has returned to the top spot. The continued success of Android, constant advancements in mobile web and app technology (including phenomena like *Pokémon Go*), and broad support from a huge community of independent users, are many of the indicators that Java will be around for a long time to come.

While it's not the only language a serious programmer needs to know, it's one of the most influential, and it's not hard to pick up. If you want to be a computer programmer, you'd do well to start with Java.

So, You Want to Be a Java Programmer?

If you want to start writing Java code, you'll need to download the **Java Development Kit (JDK)**, which meets all the basic needs for writing Java. It will give you the JVM and tools for loading, running, archiving, and debugging your code—plus many more. You can get the JDK free from Oracle's website.

Then you'll need a place to experiment. This is called an **integrated development environment (IDE)**. An IDE is like a "sandbox" for writing code—if sandboxes were equipped with cranes, backhoes, and other heavy construction equipment. An IDE will include a source code editor, a tool to automate code building, and a debugger.

You might start with Greenfoot. Greenfoot is a free IDE and runs on Mac, Windows, Linux, or Solaris computers. You can even download Greenfoot to a USB drive and run it on different computers wherever you go. Greenfoot is an excellent way for young programmers to start learning Java because it's visual: you get to see what you're building, and the learning process is structured around making fun games. Because of the visual environment, you'll see the results of your hard work quickly. You can even publish your work online. There are helpful tutorials, and other people using Greenfoot constantly post about their successes and their struggles in the IDE's online community.

Once you've learned enough in Greenfoot, you can move on to more advanced IDEs. Greenfoot was built on top of the IDE BlueJ, which is also a simple environment well-suited to beginners, though it is less visual. This is a strong IDE and has won Gosling's approval. Finally, you can move on to a professional-level IDE. Many of these are still free: some of the best-known are Eclipse and NetBeans. Others, like IntelliJ, cost money but come with additional features important for professional, high-volume developers. By the time you're ready to try one of these pro-level applications, you'll be Java-savvy, and you'll know better what you want to get out of an IDE.

Educating Yourself for a Programming Career

As you continue to get better and better with Java, you will probably take a few tutorials or other free online learning programs, and pick up tips from programmers you meet in real life and online. In high school, you might take your first programming course or join a club.

Eventually, you'll have to make a decision about college. You should know now that you don't need a computer science degree to get a job in computer programming. When StackOverflow, the internet's biggest web community of programmers, took their annual poll of community members in 2015 and asked how many had a computer science degree, the number was close to half. Very few had a PhD, and very few were over the age of forty. (This is an important lesson in statistics: the survey is an imperfect snapshot, because it doesn't account for all the programmers who don't use the website—and these are mostly older, and likelier to have college degrees.)

The roughly 50 percent of StackOverflow programmers who responded that they didn't have a computer science degree found unconventional and probably difficult paths into the industry. If you want to be a programmer and don't want to get a computer science degree, you may be shut out of certain companies altogether. Google, for example, does not currently interview candidates without computer science degrees for any engineering position. It will also be difficult to advance to an upper-level position without a degree, no matter your experience.

You might, however, get a position at a startup (a recently formed company trying to disrupt an industry)—and there are always plenty of startups in tech, with plenty of need for programmers. You can also find your way into the industry through a side door. If you have experience in computer science but get a college degree in economics, say, you could end up working for a bank, an investment firm, or a research institute, start to pick up programming work while there, and then jump to a proper tech job once you have enough experience. And there is a growing number of people in the technology and computer industries who are questioning the value of college degrees altogether. Peter Thiel, the founder of the internet payment transaction company PayPal, has a foundation that pays $100,000 each to twenty young people each year, so long as they drop out of (or delay) college to work on their technology projects.

So, it's possible to get a job in programming without a computer science degree, so long as you teach yourself, engage with other developers and make good connections, earn programming experience outside of the classroom, and confidently navigate an unusual path. By the time you're ready to make a decision about college, the industry might have changed even further. For now, though, keep in mind that for most programmer-hopefuls, a four-year computer science degree is the best way to a job.

Beyond Java: Going Multilingual

Very few programmers write in only one language. Even those whose job titles say something like "Senior Java Developer" probably work with other languages regularly. If you're interested in Java, you'll want to learn additional languages, either sooner or later, for two reasons: first, to give yourself a leg up in learning Java, and second, to make yourself more adaptable in a constantly changing field.

If you want to learn another language to ease yourself into Java, you should stick with other object-oriented languages. Anything else would only confuse you at this stage. If you have significant experience in C++, you can pick up Java easily and will probably be able to build serious programs within a week.

Another index similar to TIOBE, PyPL, measures interest in Google programming language tutorials. Java also leads here, taking 24 percent of search traffic. That means that beginner programmers (like you) are searching for Java more than any other language. It's probably not a bad idea to join them; but if you're concerned about standing out in the job market, you should consider learning a currently less popular language in which you expect to blossom.

If you're looking to pick up other relatively easy languages that could be valuable to your career, you have several options. Ruby, designed in the 1990s, is one of the easiest languages to learn. Often touted as fun, it's not just for fun and games: Ruby powers major business and entertainment websites like Hulu and Airbnb.

JavaScript and PHP are also both easy to learn, and valuable if you want to code for the web. JavaScript is useful for designing interactive elements on websites, the stuff users see, while PHP is useful for server-side functions that users don't see.

Finally, Python is a simple but useful language; its code can express concepts and instructions in fewer lines than Java or C++, and it can build just about anything. Python is most popular for research and scientific computing, but developers also used it to build parts of Pinterest and Instagram.

Learning any of these languages would expand your potential to build computer programs. They would make you a more versatile and valuable job candidate, and you could use many of them hand-in-hand with Java.

You should consider other "young" languages as well. Try to think about the languages that might be widely used in the coming years and consider picking these up now. Two languages like this are Google's Go and Apple's Swift, both rising on the TIOBE Index and polling well in StackOverflow's measure of developer interest in new languages.

Go's mascot is the Go gopher.

Google's Go is new, but it has deep roots, and its inventors are no newcomers. Ken Thompson and Rob Pike were already legends for their work at Bell Labs; together, they created the Unix operating system and each created several languages. They joined Google and a Google developer Robert Greisemer to create Go, released in 2007. These three designed Go in part to address dissatisfactions with C++. While it remains experimental even ten years after its launch, it's an increasingly popular language for its "clean" readability. You've probably encountered Go without knowing it: it powers parts of Google, Dropbox, Netflix, SoundCloud, and Uber.

Unlike the open-source and cross-platform Go, the language Swift, as an Apple invention, only works on Apple-affiliated operating systems. Released in 2014, it rose to the top ten on the TIOBE index by

2017. It is built on top of Objective-C and can run alongside Objective-C, C, and C++ in one program. Apple hopes it will replace Objective-C (which should make you hesitate if you're thinking about learning that language now). Lead developer Chris Lattner designed it to deal with or avoid common problems or bugs in other languages.

Swift may be difficult to learn after learning Java, though, because, like Java, it represents a paradigm shift. This shift is away from object-oriented programming entirely; Swift replaces this with "protocol-oriented programming." Protocols already exist in object-oriented programming: they state how unrelated objects will communicate. Instead of putting reproducible objects and their classes at the center of the programming paradigm, protocol-oriented programming puts protocols— what's "done"—at the center. Without getting too far from our subject in this book (Java, remember?) it seems that Swift could change the programming world in the coming years. It's safe to say, though, that protocol-oriented programming won't replace object-oriented programming entirely. What we have in Swift is a new kind of thinking that meets new needs, but that doesn't mean it meets "old" needs better than older languages. Market studies show that ancient C is the most commonly mentioned language in new job postings, but several different fields keep up a steady demand for Java programmers. Java will continue to meet other needs just as C, C++, and even older languages continue to have their important uses, too.

Career Prospects for Java Developers

If you're looking for a career as a Java developer, you'll probably start in Silicon Valley (a region of California south of San Francisco where tech giants and startups are clustered). Though many Sun developers left Oracle after the buyout, Oracle isn't getting rid of Java any time soon: it's still probably the company's biggest asset, and one proof of their commitment to the language is in the continuation of their lawsuit against Google. In 2013 alone, Oracle posted more than 2,300 jobs. Many of those were for Java-based software and application developers. The other major tech companies like Microsoft, Google, Dell, Cisco, Yahoo, and Sony also hire Java developers. If you work for one of these major computer companies, you could be developing major software applications that millions of computer users operate daily. If you work for Google, you could share in the advancement of Java through Android, and if you work for Oracle, you

Lights, Camera, Magic

○ ○ ○

The visual effects and computer graphics company Industrial Light & Magic has been a pioneer in Hollywood special effects for more than forty years. Their story started long ago, and depending on whom you ask, either in the Van Nuys neighborhood of Los Angeles, California, or in a galaxy far, far away ...

George Lucas's *Star Wars* came out in 1977, cashing in on the American space obsession that had started May 25, 1961, when President John F. Kennedy announced that the nation would beat the Soviets in the race to put a human on the moon. Stanley Kubrick's *2001: A Space Odyssey* became the definitive space film when Kubrick released it in 1968, just over one year before Kennedy's promise came true. Lucas may not have surpassed Kubrick's artistic achievement with *2001*, but *Star Wars* did achieve something else that Kubrick's film couldn't: it launched the great tragedies and romances of ancient Greek and Roman and medieval culture into space and has inspired each successive generation, becoming a triple trilogy and one of the world's most well-recognized franchises and most-beloved stories.

Lucas's ambitions were set high from the beginning. Inspired by Kubrick's visually stunning work, Lucas wanted to make a film that looked like nothing anyone had seen before—on a screen or off. The first *Star Wars* film (later retitled *Star Wars Episode IV: A New Hope*) didn't use much that we could call computer-generated imagery (CGI). Back then, "special effects" concerned mostly models, projection, cutting or overlaying the physical film, and work with filters and other methods of distorting camera lenses. (The few computer-

Hollywood animators need to know multiple programming languages.

generated visuals that did go into the first film were the work of programmers outside IL&M.) However, IL&M teamed up with a new group of hires (called the Computer Division of Lucasfilm, Lucas's production company) on the sequel, *Episode V: The Empire Strikes Back.* After this film and a few other contemporaries, the inevitable coming together of Hollywood and the computer industry was clear. The Computer Division broke off to become Pixar, creating the first fully CGI film, *Toy Story*, in 1995. IL&M also shifted to embrace CGI and quickly became the world's leader in that field.

Jurassic Park, Indiana Jones, Terminator, E.T.: The Extra Terrestrial, and *Pirates of the Caribbean* are just a few of more than three hundred films that have relied on IL&M for special effects, earning the company seventeen Oscar wins and twenty-three nominations. While the IL&M programmers use many languages and tools, Java was an important part of their successes. Today, many of the entry-level jobs they advertise state knowledge of Java or another major language (like C or C++) as a requirement.

Looking ahead to the next forty years of innovation, IL&M has also set up a lab for immersive and interactive entertainment experiences. If you want to become a part of the Hollywood CGI or next-generation entertainment industries, you'll have to pick up skills well beyond writing good Java code—but Java might be the smart place for you to start.

could contribute to the development and long-term health of the Java language itself. Who knows: you could even end up working for a company that buys out Oracle or buys the language. In one of the world's youngest industries, anything is possible.

One of the most common spots for Java programmers is actually outside the computer industry, in so-called big business. Today, the vast majority of Fortune 500 companies—the biggest companies in America, and some of the biggest in the world—use Java for their internal programming needs. All of those companies offer well-paid jobs to Java developers. The role of the Java developer here is in creating enterprise applications. These are software tools unlike those you find in mobile apps or installed on your home computer. Enterprise applications are massive, complicated systems critical to the functioning of large companies. These could handle billing and payroll, security, content management, secure communication within the corporation, human resources, data storage and access, and the automation of everything from manufacturing to customer service. Java is ideal for this kind of lifting, because it comes with deep, rich libraries that contain solutions for most of these standard needs. Fortune 500 corporations, unlike startups, are also generally slow to change their structural models, so they won't be switching over to

Swift anytime soon; these Java jobs will be around for a long time.

If you have a love of science, you could combine this with your passion for Java and work for an organization like NASA. We've already discussed World Wind, but NASA has used the Java language for almost all of their software, including onboard software for satellites and the latest Mars exploration rovers, and analytical programs that scientists use back on Earth. (If you're going to take this path, though, you should probably learn Python and C as well.)

Currently, the most booming field for Java is in mobile app development, and with the continued success of Android devices, that need doesn't look to be stopping any time soon. You could work for a major app development company—like Niantic, which made *Pokémon Go*; King, which made the popular game *Candy Crush*; or Rakuten, the developer behind the popular call and messaging app Viber. But with app development, you don't have to aim for a job with the giants. Plenty of popular and successful apps come from startups, or even small groups of friends who want to test their programming skills in the smartphone marketplace. If you design and release a successful Android app with your Java skills, this could lead to opportunities at many of the bigger companies named above.

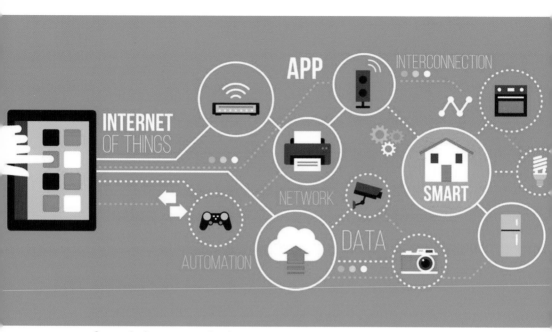

Cross-platform communication once meant computer-to-computer. Today, dozens of devices in your house alone are connected.

The Future of Java

The future of Java looks bright. Java makes up the foundation of Google's Android, one of the most popular operating systems in the world. That means that there will be a demand for hundreds of thousands of Java app developers to satisfy the cravings of more than two billion smartphone users for new tools, designs, and powers. Likewise, the trillions of dollars per year that flow through the world's biggest companies also depend, in part, on strong support for Java and its enterprise applications. Java is still easy to learn, and people new to the language still find support in an online user community of millions of Java programmers eager to share ideas and experiences, annual conferences devoted just to Java, and massive "libraries" of useful Java code others have already written.

As Gosling noted, Java's long-term success was built into its foundational principle of shared access and cross-platform communication. Today, Java owes its continued popularity to a massive user-base that crosses platforms, companies, industries, nations, and other (human) languages.

As you learned earlier, different programming languages have their strengths and weaknesses, and most end up doing different tasks. The language C powers the traffic lights that make you bring your car to a stop. Java powers the apps in the Android smartphone that you use when you're sitting in the back seat, while beside you, a friend or sibling texts on an iPhone, using Objective-C. You decide to place an order at a pizzeria near your house before you arrive there, so you pull up Google search, which uses C++ and Python, and find the pizzeria's website, which uses HTML and CSS. You click a call button built with JavaScript, and the phone begins to ring.

Soon, new languages will weave themselves into your daily life, as more and more technologies—like

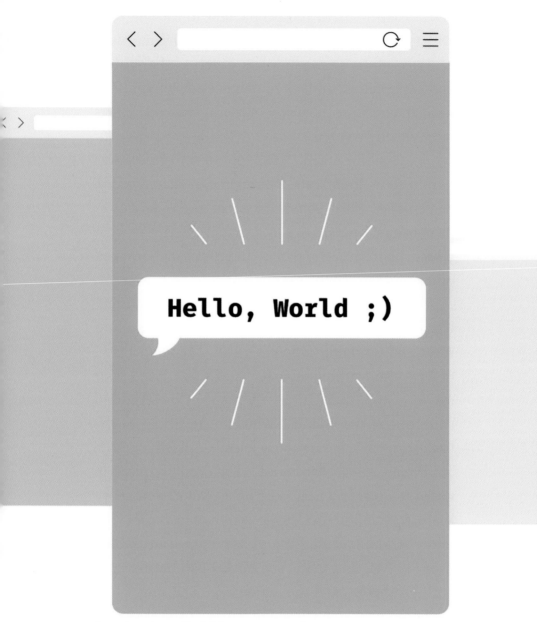

Learn how to say "hello" in any programming language—you can start with Java.

cars, refrigerators, watches, robot vacuums, and more than any of us can imagine connect to the internet, to each other, and to us. Many languages will play their specific roles in this. But as specialized as programming languages have become, there's one function that every single programming language has done, and done many, many times.

It's called "Hello, world!" If you say those two words to any programmer, she'll know what you mean. To demonstrate what a new language looks like, or to teach basic syntax to a new learner, programmers will usually write a "Hello, world!" app, displaying just that greeting. If you're going to learn Java programming, the "Hello, world!" app will be one of the first that you build, before you learn how to do much more impressive and complicated things. But really, every app you make, every line of code you write, and every new programming accomplishment you achieve will be a way of saying "Hello, world!"

So, Java programmer: now that you know about one of the most important languages to life on Earth, a language millions of people can write and billions of computers can read—though neither can speak it—it's your turn to say "Hello, world!" Say it with Java, and say it in a new way, a way that only *you* could say it. With those two words, you just might change the world you're greeting.

<Glossary/>

API Sets of instructions that allow different software programs to interact with each other; "API" stands for "application program interface."

applet A program that performs a simple task.

application Anything that performs a task, generally larger or more complex than an applet.

assembly language An assembly language is one step above machine language. Instead of 1s and 0s, assembly languages give commands using mnemonic codes like "add" and "pay."

behavior In object-oriented computer programming (OOP), things that can happen to an object, or that an object can do.

binary code A coding language that uses combinations of 1s and 0s to represent any number, letter, or other symbol to a computer.

bytecode In Java, a set of instructions that allow the Java Virtual Machine to translate any programmer's Java code to work on any operating system.

class A blueprint or template for creating objects in Java. A class identifies states and behaviors.

compiler A computer program that transforms the source code for another program into a different programming language.

computer programming language A system of written instructions for communicating data and assigning actions to computers.

GPS Global Positioning System; a technology that uses satellites to track the movement of devices—and the people that carry or ride in them—on Earth.

integrated development environment (IDE) An IDE is a software program that functions like a workshop in which to code. Most IDEs contain a source code editor, a tool that automates coding, and a debugger.

internet A global system of interconnected computers.

interoperability The ability of different languages to interact and operate upon the same data structures.

Java Development Kit (JDK) A package containing all the basic tools you need to write and run Java programs; this includes the JVM.

Java Virtual Machine (JVM) A virtual "computer" that allows Java programs to be portable, or work on any platform.

machine language Numeric codes for the operations that a given computer can execute directly; these usually consist of strings of 1s and 0s.

main A type of method in a Java app; the first or most important thing that a Java app will do.

method In Java, a method is a way of expressing an object's behaviors—what the object will do.

Mosaic An early web browser, produced by the National Center for Supercomputing Applications between 1993 and 1997, named after the art of arranging tiny pieces of glass or other colored materials.

object-oriented A term that refers to programming languages built around objects rather than actions.

objects In computer programming, an object is a pre-defined unit containing data and information. Complex coding is easier with objects.

open-source Software for which the original source code is freely available to be studied and modified.

paradigm A system of beliefs, assumptions, and attitudes that affect the way an individual or group perceives and interacts with the world.

plug-in An additional feature on an existing program, such as a search function or virus scanner on a website.

portability A programming language that can run on any platform.

scalability A way of measuring (or at least talking about) the ability of a computer, network, or program to handle many users simultaneously. A program, for example, scan scale "up" (by adding memory, etc.) or scale "out" (by adding more computers, etc.).

states In Java, characteristics of an object.

string A packet of information, or data, in many computer programming languages, including Java.

syntax A set of rules about the arrangement and interpretation of words in a sentence; or, in the case of Java, the arrangement and interpretation of classes and objects.

Virtual Network Computing (VNC) A system that allows one computer user to view and control the desktop of another, remote computer.

World Wide Web An information space using the internet to identify, organize, and link text documents, images, audio, and video.

Books

Burd, Barry A. *Android Application Development All-in-One for Dummies.* 2nd ed. Hoboken, NJ: John Wiley & Sons, Inc., 2015.

Conrod, Philip, and Lou Tyree. *Java for Kids: A Netbeans Computer Programming Tutorial.* 8th ed. Maple Valley, WA: Kidware Software, 2015.

Sierra, Kathy, and Bert Bates. *Head First Java.* 2nd ed. Sebastopol: O'Reilly Media, Inc., 2005.

Websites

BlueJ

https://www.bluej.org

Download BlueJ, one of the most popular IDEs for Java, and find resources developed by King's College of London and the University of Kent.

Greenfoot

https://www.greenfoot.org/door

Find videos, articles, and a free program tailored to Java beginners.

Young Developer – Visual Programming Software Tools

http://www.oracle.com/technetwork/topics/
newtojava/young-developers-jsp-136992.html

Explore a set of resources for learning Java, curated by Oracle.

Videos

Java Programming

https://www.youtube.com/watch?v=WPvGqX-TXP0

This fast-paced video is an overview of core Java programming skills.

Java Programming—Easy-to-Follow Java Tutorial for Beginners with Interesting Examples

https://www.youtube.com/watch?v=JPOzWljLYuU

A comprehensive, hour-long video designed for new programmers.

Allman, Eric. "A Conversation with James Gosling."
    ACMQueue, August 31, 2004. http://queue.acm.org/detail.
    cfm?id=1017013.

Bolton, David. "When and Why You Should Use C++." Dice.com,
    July 25, 2013. http://insights.dice.com/2013/07/25/who-
    uses-c-and-why/.

Carson, Erin. "Do Programmers Still Need a Computer Science
    Degree to Land a Great Job?" TechRepublic, May 20, 2014.
    http://www.techrepublic.com/article/do-programmers-still-
    need-a-computer-science-degree-to-land-a-great-job/.

Eichenwald, Kurt. "The Great Smartphone War." Vanity
    Fair, June 2014. http://www.vanityfair.com/news/
    business/2014/06/apple-samsung-smartphone-patent-war.

Gomes, Lee. "Sun Microsystems' Rise and Fall." Forbes,
    March 19, 2009. https://www.forbes.com/2009/03/18/
    sun-microsystems-internet-technology-enterprise-tech-sun-
    microsystems.html.

Gosling, James, and Henry McGilton. "The Java Language
    Environment." Oracle. Retrieved March 26, 2017. http://
    www.oracle.com/technetwork/java/hotjava-142072.html.

Handy, Alex. "Twenty Years of Java through Its Creator's Eyes."
    SD Times, May 20, 2015. http://sdtimes.com/twenty-years-
    of-java-through-its-creators-eyes/.

McMillan, Robert. "Is Java Losing Its Mojo?" *Wired*, January 8, 2013. https://www.wired.com/2013/01/java-no-longer-a-favorite/.

Miller, Michael J. "Interview with Scott McNealy." *PC Mag*, September 4, 2001. http://www.pcmag.com/article2/0,2817,35769,00.asp.

Murphy, Kieron. "So Why Did They Decide to Call It Java?" *JavaWorld*, October 4, 1996. http://www.javaworld.com/article/2077265/core-java/so-why-did-they-decide-to-call-it-java-.html.

Sierra, Kathy, and Bert Bates. *Head First Java*. 2nd ed. Sebastopol, CA: O'Reilly Media, Inc., 2005.

Smith, Jacquelyn. "The 25 Tech Companies Hiring the Most Right Now." *Forbes*, April 4, 2013. https://www.forbes.com/sites/jacquelynsmith/2013/04/04/the-25-tech-companies-hiring-the-most-right-now/#603a781a19b6.

Stafford-Fraser, Quentin. "The Trojan Room Coffee Pot." The Computer Laboratory. University of Cambridge, May 1995. https://www.cl.cam.ac.uk/coffee/qsf/coffee.html.

Taft, Darryl K. "Java Creator James Gosling: Why I Quit Oracle." eWeek, September 22, 2010. http://www.eweek.com/development/java-creator-james-gosling-why-i-quit-oracle.

Tajnai, Carolyn. "Sun Microsystems Spotlight." Stanford University. Retrieved April 10, 2017. http://web.stanford.edu/group/wellspring/sun_spotlight.html.

Tsukayama, Haley. "Pokemon Go's Unexpected Side Effect: Injuries." *The Washington Post*, July 10, 2016. https://www.washingtonpost.com/news/the-switch/wp/2016/07/08/pokemon-gos-unexpected-side-effect-injuries/?utm_term=.d6a400c6de0f.

Wielenga, Geertjan. "Developing NASA's mission software with Java." Jaxenter, September 23, 2014. https://jaxenter.com/netbeans/developing-nasas-mission-software-with-java.

Zakhour, Sharon, et. al. *The Java Tutorial Fourth Edition: A Short Course on the Basics.* Boston: Pearson Education, Inc., 2006.

Aidan M. Ryan is a writer, publisher, and educator based in Buffalo, New York. His features, reviews, interviews, and essays have appeared in the *White Review*, *Traffic East*, *Buffalo News*, *The Skinny*, and on CNN; his poetry has appeared recently in *The Honest Ulstermann*, *Slipstream*, *Ghost City Review*, and *Peach Mag*. He works in marketing and is also an adjunct professor of English at Canisius College and a Teaching Artist at the Just Buffalo Writing Center. Aidan is managing editor of the poetry magazine *Foundlings* and is the author of *Organizing Isolation: Half-Lives of Love at Long Distance*, a collection of visual poetry published by Linoleum Press in April 2017.